NO MAP COULD SHOW THEM

BY THE SAME AUTHOR

Division Street

NO MAP COULD SHOW THEM

Helen Mort

Chatto & Windus
LONDON

1 3 5 7 9 10 8 6 4 2

Chatto & Windus, an imprint of Vintage,
20 Vauxhall Bridge Road,
London SW1V 2SA

Chatto & Windus is part of the Penguin Random House
group of companies whose addresses can be found at
global.penguinrandomhouse.com.

Penguin
Random House
UK

First published by Chatto and Windus in 2016

www.vintage-books.co.uk

A CIP catalogue record for this book is
available from the British Library

ISBN 9781784740641

Typeset by Palimpsest Book Production Limited, Falkirk, Stirlingshire
Printed and bound in Great Britain by Clays Ltd, St Ives plc

Penguin Random House is committed to a sustainable future
for our business, our readers and our planet. This book is made
from Forest Stewardship Council® certified paper.

MIX
Paper from
responsible sources
FSC
www.fsc.org   FSC® C018179

For Ben, who catches my falls.

'*Suffering is above, not below. And everyone thinks that suffering is below. And everyone wants to rise.*'
—ANTONIO PORCHIA, 1943,
trans. W. S. Merwin

Contents

NO MAP COULD SHOW THEM

No map can show you
but you're in every line.

There: like the underground stream
and the once-worked mine.

You're the last fence in England,
everything most-northerly.

Your scale's unknowable,
your permanence is watery.

You're as thin as a bulrush,
as scattered as rapeseed –

your body a contour line
we once knew how to read.

Due west, due east, you are
x-marks-the-spot.

We plot you from memory
with our eyes tight shut.

You're a reference with no grid,
the point sea forgets land.

I know you at arm's length,
like the back of my hand.

Mountain

You are very successful
but you have rocks in your chest,

skin-coloured sandstone
wedged where your breasts should be.

Your stomach is a boulder.
To hold you up, your legs grow stony too.

You zip your jacket up
and nobody notices you are a mountain.

You buy coffee,
run board meetings where no-one says

you're made of scree
but above your head, their talk is weather,

your eyes collect new rain
and you know what you are because

like any hillside
you don't sleep. Your feet could hold you here

forever but your sides
are crumbling, and when you speak

your words are rockfall, you're
scared your heart is tumbling from your mouth.

An Easy Day for a Lady

'The Grepon has disappeared. Of course, there are still some rocks standing there, but as a climb it no longer exists. Now that it has been done by two women alone, no self-respecting man can undertake it.'
— ETIENNE BRUHL, 1929

When we climb alone
en cordée feminine,
we are magicians of the Alps –
we make the routes we follow
disappear.

Turn round
to see the swooping absence
of the face, the undone glaciers,
crevasses closing in on themselves
like flowers at night.

We're reeling in the sky.
The forest curls into a fist.
The lake is no more permanent
than frost. Where you made ways,
we will unmake:

give back the silence
at the dawn of things.
Beneath your feet,
the ground
retracts its hand.

How to Dress

'A lady's dress is inconvenient for mountaineering.'
– MRS HENRY WARWICK COLE, 1859

Your fashionable shoes
might be the death of you.

Your hemline catches stones
and sends them plummeting.

Below the col, set down your parasol,
put on the mountain's suit –

your forearms gloved with permafrost,
your fingers lichen-light,

your mouth becoming fissured
and your ankles malachite.

Slip on a jacket made of shale,
cold stockings from a forded stream.

Take off the clothes they want
to keep you in. The shadow of the hill

undresses you. The sky
will be your broad-brimmed hat.

Miss Jemima's Swiss Journal

after Jemima Morrell and her tour of the Alps, 1863

Each summer I'll be Miss Jemima,
snug in my temperance
and crinoline,

taking chocolate in Grindelwald,
the Eiger flashing down
stern looks.

I'll be devastating in my notebooks,
reserve my best scorn
for the tour guide

with his winter field of hair,
the tittering ladies in the gardens
near Reichenbach.

I think I could get used to it –
the chastity
and limp green vegetables

as long as I could stand in my blue dress
beneath the falls
at Lauterbrunnen, higher

than all society, a teardrop
if you only saw me
from the sky.

Ode to Bob

'Then there is 'Bob', the imaginary character invented by women climbers tired of hearing unsolicited advice from male passersby...' – DAVID MAZEL, 1994

For he never calls to us unkindly
from a ledge, voice like an avalanche.

His feet dislodge no flat-backed stones.

For when he drinks, he leaves the whisky
undiminished in the flask.

He never steals the morning
with a story of a pitch he climbed
one handed, wearing boxing gloves

and never casts his shadow
on the path, dark as a winter coat,

nor whistles like a postman
from his belay stance.

For, when he has advice
he will not offer it

and when we have advice
he takes no heed.

The rain stitching
the valley does not trouble him,

the wind can never peel his body
from the crag.

For I will not have to
love him,

watch as he threads
a way through limestone,

finding the day's vanishing point.

Height

Fanny Bullock Workman jumps a crevasse
above the Hispar, Karakorum

I hated that leap,
by matchless dark,
across four feet, invisible.

It was only
a bed's width, only
an arm span, less than my height.

I seemed so light
I might not land again;
go clear above the seracs

and the frozen scarps,
hopscotch the stars, hurdle
the amber moon by accident.

Just for a breath, I flew,
afraid you could not anchor me,
the earth not bring me back.

The Fear

I worried about running. My fear grew legs and raced me to the finish line. I worried about finishing and my fear was lacquered, shone: that fruit-sized model of the globe I wanted as a kid. I turned it in my sleep – distant countries, oceans I couldn't name. I worried about my name and fear introduced itself before me at the party. I worried about the party and fear was a drink, a pale flute pushed into my hand. I worried about drink, so fear leaked through the seams of my clothes, grew into a stain on my wool coat and people pretended not to look. See – I'm still standing in the corner where you left me, mid-sentence. I've promised not to move, but of course I'm worried about my promise and fear is a pledge, a lifelong IOU, a signature that looks like this.

Scale

My weight is
four whippets,

two Chinese gymnasts,
half a shotputter.

It can be measured
in bags of sugar, jam jars,

enough feathers for 60 pillows,
a flock of dead birds

but some days it's more
than the house, the span

of Blair Athol Road.
I'm The Crooked Spire

warping itself,
looming over town.

I measure myself against
the sky in its winter coat,

peat traces in water, air
locked in the radiators at night,

against my own held breath,
or your unfinished sentences,

your hand on my back
like a passenger

touching the dashboard
when a driver brakes,

as if to slow things down.
I measure myself against

love – heavier, lighter
than both of us.

Beryl the Peril

In my badly-drawn version,
Beryl is getting shit-faced
with Desperate Dan,

matching him
with every dripping forkful
of cow pie.

Beryl is outsprinting
store detectives, hurdling
the trolleys outside Sainsbury's.

Her plaits are strings
of sausages. Her thought bubbles
are crammed with asterisks.

Beryl has an oak-tree waist
and knitted eyebrows,
a jaw

like a paperweight.
I watch her turn into her namesake,
my grandmother –

her crumpled spine,
her folded lung
her punctured smile,

my gran, who chased her brother
with a pickaxe handle, watched
her father gas himself,

who'd draw the final frames
if only she could
grip the pen – Beryl

clambering from the page
reaching the greatest height, gobbing
on us all.

My Diet

My diet comes with a free fork. You use it
to puncture yourself like a barbecue sausage
so all the wasted breath comes out of you,
like this. Mine is the Shackleton Diet, you eat
your boots. The Everest Diet, where frostbite
lightens your extremities. On my diet, you can eat
but only with your eyes shut. My diet
is like the wheel of a very small bicycle,
rotating fast. It's the colander diet: you pick
out the gaps and eat them. My diet is
the South Yorkshire Coalfields diet.
It includes nothing but a small apology.
On my diet, you can eat your own
past, very carefully, like nibbling the corner
of a photograph. My diet is the Diet of Worms.
You can only eat religious assemblies
from the sixteenth century. My diet is
the diet of a dancer who can't dance.
My diet is bigger than your diet and that's
what scares me. My diet is self-sustaining.
If you like, you may begin
to eat yourself, slowly,
starting from inside.

Difficult

'God knows there are difficult women out there.
Women who are – at times – shallow, bitchy, selfish,
dishonest and, of course, crazy.'
   – ASKMEN: WHY MEN DATE DIFFICULT WOMEN

Difficult women don't care what time it is, they're
crowding the bus stop with their difficult bodies,
refusing to budge for the light, or in the parks,
dragging their difficulty behind them like a fat dog.
Some of them are running, cycling, or worse,
driving cars. If a difficult woman hits you at 30 miles per hour
you have a 50 percent chance of survival. At home,
difficult women are more like walls than windows
but if you lean on one, you fall straight through
and sometimes at night they show your face.

Difficult women don't know they're born.
Difficult women don't know the meaning of the word.
There could be one folded into your newspaper,
holding her breasts like oranges. There might be
one carrying your coffee, or moving to your road.
In London, it's said you're never more than 6 feet
from a difficult woman. Have you or a colleague
had a difficult woman in the last 6 months?
If so, you may be entitled to compensation.
Do you have difficulty with our questions?
Are you afraid you may be difficult yourself?

The Old Dungeon Ghyll

That bird, battering the corners of the Dungeon Ghyll,
rain scattered like confetti from its wings
and the pub divided: those who tried to swoop for it
and others, too afraid to move.
We froze inside our soaking clothes. Sometimes
I'd think to touch you, stop myself.

Behind us was the wooden table, scored with signatures
where I once tried to carve my name
and nicked my wrist, the penknife shaking
till the barman took my hand:
If you have to leave a mark, don't make it shit.
I tried again, half meaning it.

Hill

Each time I think of you, you're halfway up a hill you've never
climbed before. Autumn, the Calder Valley chimneys breathing light,

the beech trees mimicking a corner of night – black trunks,
the spans between them tiny measures of the sky.

Up here, the walks you haven't taken grow precise,
undone and certain, tightening like the hand of the day.

Although I'm seven hills away, I'd like to tell you
somewhere on the map there must be plains

we do not know about, towns with names no-one can list,
and ordinary, hidden lakes, a single cloud shaped nothing like a leaf.

I mean to say there must be better ways of putting things,
unwritten routes, stone-knuckled paths to overshoot, words

practised till they come out rough. And from this height,
and on this tilted Yorkshire earth it seems enough.

Black Rocks

i.m Alison Hargreaves, 1963–1995

Descent

Abseiling down from Tryfan
in the growing dark –
thirteen, your braking hand
tight on the rope –

you move through
hills that seem to swarm
at you, the cattle cry
with voices from another world

and at the base,
you keep descending
through your own short life –
the rope becomes

the one you inched down
in the Alps, the Himalayas,
landscapes hunched
in shelter from the sky

and every rock
you pass might be
a face, hidden
by starlessness,

though as you stare at them,
they freeze again,
the whole world's still
except for you:

parting the makeshift
curtain of the night
and gliding
through.

Prayer

Give us good days.
Days unspectacular but adequate:
the weather neither calm nor wild,
your coat zipped nearly to the top,

a silver thermos cooling in your bag,
the sky at Bamford reddening, as if
embarrassed by its own strange reach
and day-old, pipe-smoke clouds.

Above the Hope cement works,
crows wheel arcs of guarded flight
and when you touch the rock
your fingers hold.

Kiss

'A few weeks after her first rock climb, Alison kissed a boy for the first time. Unlike her climbing, the event was recorded in her diary without detail or comment.'
– ED DOUGLAS AND DAVID ROSE, 1999

But why record
that unexpected warmth,

your lips as vague as his,
his face becoming yours,

the way you noticed
every tooth inside his mouth?

How could you write
that you weren't sure

whether to close your eyes,
and, when you did,

you felt suspended
in thin air?

It came to this: your hot,
over-familiar breath, the taste

of his stale chewing-gum,
your hands clamped to your sides,

and you, for the first time,
not knowing what to do with them.

Solo

And as you climbed,
you clambered from your own taut skin
and watched yourself, amused:

the mushroom of your woollen hat,
your top lip starred with blood,
your bitten fingernails.

It seemed so easy, looking on –
you yelled instructions to yourself,
laughed when she slipped

and while she held the slopers,
you were free, auditioning
to be the high, indifferent sun,

the second pitch, its poker face,
the ground, waiting
to catch or break.

Nordwand

Below The White Spider
you clench yourself into a ball,
your unborn child held deep inside.

You wish that you could reach
beneath your skin
and hold the baby's fist in yours

but you can only curl
into the Eiger's mists, cupped
in a belly of enfolding snow,

stiff-limbed, as if the cold
could cradle you, your eyes
bright glass, the wind a lullaby,

its calm voice calling you
into the world, and stonefall
answering *not yet*.

Home

'Oh, a woman is so missing snow, ice, rock...'
– ENTRY IN ALISON'S DIARY, EARLY 1978,
AFTER BREAKING HER LEG

Even in your house you aren't at home –
your blue raincoat collapsing from its peg,
teacups abandoned in the kitchen sink.

Your photos frame a girl you hardly recognise,
the form suggested in the windowpane is not
your own. Blackbirds sketch private, airy maps outside

and, in the breeze, the saplings point away from you.
You want to smash the bathroom mirror
and replace it with a sheet of ice,

take up the patterned rugs and carpet every room
with snow. Instead, you sit.
Your heart: a compass, magnetised.

At Night

That dream again: you're crouching
underneath the kitchen table. Midnight
and the moon's a fingernail.
Its silver light could cut your cheek.

You're gearing up – your harness,
crampons, heated gloves
but even when you're ready,
you don't go. You have forgotten

how to climb, can only crawl
across the floor. Upstairs,
your child's cry gathers
like an avalanche.

You wake, sit tight.
You whisper *mummy's here*.
Till dawn, your shadow
scales the walls.

Above Cromford

Your body tight against the cold
inside a tent high on K2

you dream about Black Rocks:
squat monoliths, tattooed with names,

routes so graffitied
that you'd sink your fingers

into letters, pull
on the initials of the dead.

You didn't need to carve your own.
Your signature was grip and lift,

partnerless dance that left
no mark, and as you moved

the sequences spelled out
your name. And it was

unrepeatable. And gone
when you looked back.

Routes

You might have died
where the road kicks back on itself
and the rain lies black
against the tarmac, barely glistening.

Or met with lightning
in a field watched only by
three knuckled trees, your figure
brief, joined to the sky.

Or simply counted out
your allocated breaths
your numbered heartbeats
in an ordinary room

and never seen
the Karakoram opening,
the clouds finding their shapes
beneath your feet.

Dear Alison

When I make slow patterns
on a route called Namenlos
I'm writing to you –

late afternoon
and Stanage is a postcard to your loss,
stamped with a daytime moon.

The midges are small handwriting.
Below, my friends lean
intricate as lettering.

I write to you
because your imprint's everywhere
across the landscape's leaned-on page.

I know I'll never climb
as high as you, or hold my nerve

and you'd have laughed
to see my tight-knit fears.

I understand the curve
of one low edge can be enough
to spend a lifetime on

and if you'd had a lifetime,
maybe you'd have turned
to face Apparent North,

this long, abandoned storyline,
maybe you'd have picked up where we all
leave off.

Engineer

The night takes everything
except a railway engineer,
alone on the tracks with his lamp –

its beam shows nothing,
it must be the dream of a lamp.
The rails sing quietly as he walks.

Somewhere, there is a town
where all the lights will burn
till he comes home.

Lethal Roy

for Brendan Cleary

He's the dog you never
bet on, the one who
always, nearly, might have, will…

The one who steals the show
while no-one's watching,
outrunning surprise,

or doesn't even have to run,
stitching the race up
from his kennel bed.

Dead afternoons, he pads
down the home straight,
his shadow half a pace ahead.

He's the name traced
in the phone directory
twenty years too late,

the face seen for
a second on the train,
not shaken since.

When he runs,
his breathing's everything
you never said,

his fur the colour
of the last great snow,
or the colour of nothing.

Bloodhound

'As to goodbye, not much
to be said for it.'
   – KEN SMITH, 'Fox Running'

She follows disappointing scents
from dusk to dusk,
liver and tan,

circling the city's rim,
someone driving past their own
house, afraid to go in.

She catches her death
on the evening wind that scuffs
the tops of trees, lifts up the bins

and gives slow chase: death
on the billboard model with her beautiful
cargo of limbs,

death in the man who rides
the 26 to Hackney Wick, out
from the depot, back again,

death in the dark strip
of the old canal that underlines
her route downtown,

death in the folds of city boys
in tailored suits who hold
their matching pints, death

sheltering in shop doorways
or walking home in shirtsleeves
with his coat off,

death asking for small change
and death giving it out, pockets
always deep enough.

Death following the stockmarket.
Death locking the door
in a boutique hotel.

She sniffs it out, again, again
and can't think what
to do with it and carries on,

catching an interfering scent,
half-criminal, half-animal
and loping down the thoroughfares,

the Thames an interruption
in the night, her trail leading across
the bridge that shook and never

fell. Nobody blocks her way.
Nobody tries to leash her to their side.
Nobody handles her.

You've seen her with her heavy stride,
her sagging chin, the dumbbells
of her paws.

She's middle-aged, invisible.
She isn't known to raise her voice, her yap
kept buried in her wrinkled chest,

her flesh shortlived. O but they'd say
her bones are artefacts, shaped
over centuries, outlasting rot

and though she is too old to bleed,
her snout's so keen she smells
each drop before it forms, before

it falls, smells it on the teenage girl
who rides the Hammersmith and City,
her legs crossed tight,

smells it on the boy
who walks through Shoreditch
cauterised, his hand against his chest.

She goes unnoticed, down
through Crooked Usage, Long Acre,
Accommodation Lane. She runs

nose to the ground, dislodging chicken bones,
the damp, unwanted pages of old news.
She follows notes of piss and whisky

till they peter out, rare places
where the street's washed clean again,
gutters where the trail runs underground.

You run with the hare
and you hunt with the hounds.
That was always her trouble, always

what troubled her,
her kind set loose to bring back slaves
some other century, or chase a fox

to stillness in the woods.
And part of her escaping
with the uncaught prey, part of her

loosed, part of her
run to ground. *You hunt with the hare*
and you run with the hounds.

She's fickle and sincere.
She has outlived her use,
but sharpens at a whiff of fear,

your dread, her dread, his dread,
ours. She's the bailiff calling
out of hours, in black now, lovely,

raising herself to her full height,
listing everything you owe. You lie dead
still and listen for her in the night.

Knock knock. Who's there?
It's Nothing. Nothing who?
Knock knock. It's Nothing. You.

Skirt

A found poem drawn from Wikipedia: '1920s in Western Fashion', and an online forum discussing the mini skirt

For the first time in centuries
women's legs were seen
with hemlines rising to the knee.

They are too short
it makes men want to go up their skirts
I am 60 years old do you agree?

Knife-pleated skirts
low-waisted dresses, letting
women quite literally kick up their heels.

I too am past it
and still want to go up women's skirts
I know how that feels

Proper attire for women
was enforced for morning, afternoon activities,
adorned with sashes, artificial flowers at the waist.

I know we enjoy it
however it ruins our summer
and I am tired, you can't look at their face

A more masculine look
including flattened breasts and hips
short hairstyles like the Marcel Wave, the Eton Crop.

I don't go out of my way to stare
down her top, it's just we get out of focus
and then we fail our exam

Marcel Grateau. Francois Marcel.
Given the dates, it's quite
possible they were all the same man.

Rachel in Attercliffe

I'm in suspenders, working Boxing Day.
Your dad, your boyfriend nips out for a beer
then indicates down Derek Dooley Way.
The sign outside says *entrance at rear*.
There's tinsel round the bannister, a star
above each bedroom door. I'm crimson to my hips.
I let them lift the layers and unhook my bra.
They're talkative, telling me what the kids
got yesterday. I smile. I don't mention my son.
Sometimes, I say I work in mental health.
The ones who're silent when they come
intrigue me most. You have to laugh at yourself.
I like to think there's hospital, a recently-dead wife.
I like to think I'm saving someone's life.

King's Cross

The man who needs money
says I ought to be a film star
and that you'd better look after me.

I want to ask if he means
a Hitchcock movie
or a nineties horror film

but he's showing his stabbed wrist,
the paperweight of his closed fist,
telling us what meds they keep him on.

And yes, we look like a crap film set,
me on the piano stool, one shoe off,
you sitting on the concourse floor

and all we can give is small change.
Later, our train missed, I'll be like a kid,
saying *the world's a bad place*

and you'll tell me that it isn't
and we'll both be right
and fall asleep in the single bed

of the dim hotel
where *guests may be ejected*
for unacceptable dress

and I'll be the film of your body,

you'll be the film of mine
and on the next-day train

I'll watch everything pass,
everything approach
in your eyes.

Ink

Harder to see your blood
than take the ink myself:

you, upright in the leather chair
and Tom-Lee leaning close

scarring you elegantly, gradually
with a dark-winged bird

that means Liverpool.
Tattooing is like love

an idiot tried to tell me once.
You have to close your eyes

and let it pass.
Your skin is crimson, raw.

I'll never close my eyes to you.
Not now or afterwards,

those weeks of healing
and me, wanting to touch you

there
an inch above the heart.

What Will Happen

for Kathrine Switzer

If I run too far, too quickly, my breasts
will drop to my kneecaps and my uterus will fall out.

My light hair will grow heavy,
My hips will drag along the floor.

Don't I know the rules of gravity?
Didn't they teach me what my body was

at school? I should be stowed
away from direct sunlight, saved from rain.

Who told me it was possible
to run out of my skin,

outsprint the stewards,
on the Boston sidewalk

breathless, waiting
for the world to catch up?

Ablation

Inside the Northern General
they're trying to burn away
a small piece of your heart.

I want to know which bit,
how much
and what it holds.

My questions live
between what doctors call the heart
and what we mean by it,

wide as the gap between brain and mind.
And in our lineage of bypassed hearts
we should be grateful

for the literal. I know my heart
is your heart – good for running,
not much else

and later as you sit up in your borrowed bed
I get the whole thing wrong,
call it *oblation*. Offering

or sacrifice. As if you'd given something up.
As if their tiny fire was ritual
and we could warm by it.

Hathersage

It's the night robin, near midnight,
singing in bad weather. Or the thought
that snow could shore us until Spring.
How twilight makes the moors half-luminous
and the man in the post office knows you by voice.

It's hard to say a thing simply,
but here, the sun manages it,
a flashbulb through the branches
taking your photograph
all the way out of town.

Kalymnos

The rock took all my fingerprints from me.
Below the crag, I watched a man lie down
beneath a canopy of leaves and die.

The bush was starred with wide pink
flowers – by night they'd smell of marzipan.
The shade passed a hand over his shape.

We climbed beside our shadows
through the afternoon, always one move ahead.
When there was nothing left, we came down.

The bay was a lidless eye. As I got close,
the dead man gathered himself up, replaced
his hat and walked away.

Loutro

I couldn't stop thinking about the mad goat,
marooned on the uninhabited island,
how it fattened on the feed
the owners hauled to it by boat –
barrage balloon on spindly legs.
It had a favourite auntie's name.
Before its exile, it broke rooftops
and men's bodies with its hooves.

When I swam as far as I dared, it was there:
high on an outcrop, rock-coloured,
unmoved. It watched me, flailing
for the shore, staring me down
with empty, human eyes.

II

The parrot with its docked wings and clipped
tail feathers could meow like a spoiled cat
or screech like a child. It perched on top
of its cage and wolf-whistled for sport,
making the ex-pats blush. Occasionally,
it did the shrill pitch of a telephone.
Sometimes it shrugged as if to shake
free of its grey-pink down.

When the boat arrived with *Daskalogiannis*
painted on the prow, it shrieked –
the man they tortured in Heraklion,
the shipbuilder they say kept silent
while his captors peeled his skin off
like a good, ripe fruit.

Alport Castles

for J.W.

The wind let the landscape move
how it always wanted to,

leaned us together
like ferns, or upper branches

and we walked the slope
believing we were part of the scenery

talking about music and summits,
places we'd never go again.

Then the rocks finished my sentence –
tall and architectural:

their moat of grass
their keep of clouds,

more intricate than any human fort.
We sat up high and praised

like two off-duty gods
as if a view was something

made. And the clouds
over Derwent mended

and we were briefly glorious,
though neither of us had

built, would build a single thing.

Eagle Owl, Royal Mile

if its satchel-coloured eyes
could be bought
admit it
you would

if the autumn of its
plumage could be
gathered in
you would

if you could follow
its gaze

not the glance
from keeper's glove
to coins
from rain
to audience

but that further
days deep
runway stare

you would long
to be its shadow
you would beg for air

and it would look straight through you
for a moment
as if you were there.

Kinder Scout

Gold light. I wish the day
could break me like an egg

so I'd ooze the same colour, flatten
on the skillet of Mam Tor.

I'd like the summit path to be a knife
that pared me, skin

like apple skin, saving
just my necessary parts.

Surely the best northwesterly
could whip me into lightness,

sugar me, admit the air
so something of this landscape

could be folded in:
September bracken, lichen, stone.

I don't know if I'm ready
to be taken

but I'd like to lie prepared:
unnoticed, important as butter,

softening
on the hill's plate.

Murmuration

The bones of a daytime moon
then the shock of them across it:

using their arms like wings,
wheeling above Middleton Moor

now as one body,
now as many.

They fly in wax jackets
and blue-checked shirts,

plaid jumpers and high-vis,
magpie-black leather.

Sometimes you might catch
a bracelet falling like a feather,

feel the plumage of a skirt,
the down of a coat brush close

or crane your neck to the burr
of a word in a language you don't know

or one you've spoken all your life,
not recognised the song of it.

But mostly they stay close
together, crowding the sky,

flocking from everywhere;
Bradford and Bruges.

Retford and Romania,
from yesterday's news

and tomorrow's grainy footage.
They have seen your borders

and crossed them
the only way they can,

in the only way left to them,
rising to cloud-height,

leaving the checkpoint world,
the branches and gateposts below.

Big Lil

i.m. Lillian Bilocca and the Hull triple trawler disaster, 1968

Lil's dream

I dreamed Hessle Road was a river
thundering by night to the North Sea

and all the men I'd tried to warn
were channelled from their pubs and houses

fists still clutching glasses, papers,
kitchen knives. I lay down in the waters

like a boat, but I was buffeted,
I zig-zagged after them, face-down,

my body bloated in the stream. I could still see
and knew the shoals beneath weren't fish

but scraps of hulls and decks,
dead radios. The riverbed was lined

with messages, scribbled goodbyes
to everything we'd not yet lost

to all we could not carry, would not need
where water planned on taking us.

What the papers said

We'll fight for our lads said 17-stone Lil,
proud on the docks like a 17-stone anchor.
Each ship needs a working radio, said the fishwife,
raising herself to her full height
and full 17 stone.

Lil is meeting Harold Wilson next week
and, at 17 stone, she's bound to make an impact.
The 17-stone Hull woman has called for a reform
of fishing laws in her distinctive Yorkshire accent,
standing at 17 stone and 5 foot 5.

With 17 stone behind her, she's looking squarely
to the future. *I'm proud of her,* said her husband,
10-stone Charlie, gazing out to sea.

Lil's answer

Don't speak until you're spoken to.
The ocean's given me my cue.

You shouldn't raise your voice outdoors.
My words live in the crowd's applause.

This is a matter for the men. Go home.
I'll stand until I'm frozen down to bone.

Your accent's making you a laughing stock.
Long as they listen, let them mock.

They'll mute you, Lil. They'll throw you out to sea.
They'll have to gag this town to silence me.

Lil's last word

Nothing touches Hull except the sea.
As if a tide cut Hessle Road
and Anlaby, making us islands to ourselves.

I dived in where the ocean shelved away
and tried to swim. Before I'd raised my arms
I was already too far in

and too far out. The city fixed me
with its lighthouse stare. I opened my mouth
and I was ransacked by its glare.

I let a single word go like a flare
and watched it douse the night, then fall.
I sank as if I never swam at all.

Tom Hulatt's Mile

i.m. Tom Hulatt, 1930–1990

When the tape was broken and the clock
froze Bannister and Brasher, crowned
with sweat and round applause,
the man who really finished third

kept running, out of Iffley Road and Oxford,
north to Tibshelf: overground at first, then down
through the pit shafts and tunnels he'd worked,
earth his only audience.

He ran right out of 1954, through all the jobs
he ever had, the Derbyshire he knew.
He ran through centuries of rain
and bad ideas, through lifetimes of good luck.

Sometimes his shadow lagged behind.
He ran like weather. He ran like time.
And they call it a mile, but it lasts forever.
You can try to catch him, but there is no line.

Heinrich Harrer's Motorbike

From the horned handles down
it is a hero bike, a Nazi bike,
depending how you look. You stare
all day, killing time before your climb.

At night, you think of it: warming
its dead engine, smashing the walls,
speeding back to the Nordwand,
Mordwand, where trains now pass,

and a dozen men died tunnelling.
You imagine it arcing clean
above the Swallow's Nest,
the Hinderstoisser traverse,

the Kleine Sheidegg window –
past every tragedy you pored over
in books: the ghost of Tony Kurz
still hanging on his rope.

It rears over the White Spider,
the summit Harrer claimed.
It looks down on your dreams
of following. It does not stop,

becomes a thought, a selfishness
put out of mind, revving
in the early hours, filling the dawn.
It only lives because you let it.

How Much Can You Carry?

after a piece by Jemima Diki Sherpa

I can carry a man,
as much air as you like
caught and held in a can.

I gather each morning
in my arms
and lug the day up high.

I have shouldered
your hopes, your oldest fears,
the path I cleared

is a diagram of need.
You ask me to lift your country
as if it's light.

You have packed your history,
rivers and houses
tight. Sometimes I stand

on the summit
pretend to raise the daylight moon
on my open hand.

I have carried the lot.
Now, what should I do with it?
When do I stop?

Everest

*'Mountains are not fair or unfair,
they are just dangerous.'* – REINHOLD MESSNER

Oxygen

First you are air itself,
caught and contained
inside an orange can.
You're what remains of breath,
wide as a hand and heavier
than you look. You have a mask
and tube. Men move
with what you first mistook
for tenderness, putting their lips
to you and drawing deep.
By dark, they stare wide eyed
and sleep is held in something else
that can't be carried here.
Instead of it, they keep you near.

Beck Weathers

Are you the man who got up blind
and walked out of the grave
the snow had dug for you? Time
shivered in the space you'd made.
It might have been a year you walked.
An hour. A lost weekend.
A night without an end. Not seeing,
there was nothing you could fear
and everything you couldn't touch
was briefly near – the eye-holes
of the stars, indifferent gloom.
The mountain shrank into a room,
whose walls have kept you since.
You are awake. Sit up. Blink.

Sherpa

Your Sherpa is a dead man
but you wouldn't know, except
for when he turns, stiff as a marionette
and shows his caved-in cheek,
the flesh that paid the debt.
Of course, he cannot speak –
words go first, long before breath –
but he is ripe for tracking
and you follow him in sleep
past body markers, cased in ice.
One is your brother, one your wife,
then, at the top, bones that map yours.
Your tent flaps wide. A moment.
Then the wind's applause.

Lene Gammelgaard

Now you're a woman and that's all
they'll know, no matter
what you carry or how far
you go, alone, in rationed light.
Behind you, there must be
a mother, wringing her slim hands.
A husband who understands.
A house, two children held
in the imagined door. You are
less after than before. You'll never be
what you are now, a silence, framed
by sun. You are what's said.
You'll never be what's done.

First

You are the oldest, the youngest,
the first man to descend on skis.
The tallest, the fastest, the first
amputee, or the quietest party,
the hundredth one-of-a-kind.
To be remembered now,
you must get to the top
and leave your skin behind,
or climb with both your hands tied,
be the first walking skeleton
with snow filling your ribs, slow,
filling your eye-sockets, fast
but you'll be first, first, first
until the last.

Rope

In the dream, there's still
a rope between us.

I know it by its warp;
the careful rope you used
to bind me at the breaking points
of my body – wrists
and ankles, fastened tight,
as if to keep me to myself;

rope you fixed
to anchor us to cliffs
in case your footholds gave
or I reached to pull against
a sloping door of rock
and opened it. Rope

that knew so much
of waiting; the floorboards
cold against my spine,
or outside, listening for the call
to climb – the slack brought in
the route set out before me.

Tonight, I'm bound to you again.
We've got so high, the city's turned
to patchwork. The rope's around
my waist, the other end
around your neck so tight
you'd barely know where flesh

begins. I grip the frame,
my knuckles white. I hold my breath
on every spur of rock.
You are running for the drop,
you're gathering speed,
you're sprinting for the break.

It will be years before
I feel the catch, and wake.

Notes

'Miss Jemima's Swiss Journal' – In 1863, 31-year-old Jemima Morrell from Yorkshire embarked on one of Thomas Cook's earliest tours to Switzerland. Her account of the adventure – on foot across The Alps in a crinoline dress – was later published as *Miss Jemima's Swiss Journal*. In 2013, I repeated some of her journey.

'Black Rocks' – This sequence is dedicated to the memory of Alison Hargreaves (1963–1995), a climber from Belper, Derbyshire. Alison soloed all the great north faces of the Alps in a single season, climbed Everest unsupported in 1995 and died later that year descending from the summit of K2. Pregnant with her first child when she climbed the North Face of the Eiger, she was criticised by the press as a mountaineering mother. Her biography, *Regions of the Heart*, by David Rose and Ed Douglas was published in 1999, and details her life and the controversy surrounding her death.

'Bloodhound' – This poem was written as a response to Ken Smith's poem 'Fox Running' and based on archival research into his materials at the University of Leeds.

'Rachel in Attercliffe' – A fictional, dramatic monologue in response to a Channel 4 documentary about City Saunas in Attercliffe, Sheffield.

'What Will Happen' – On April 19th, 1967, Kathrine Switzer ran the Boston marathon, a race only open to men. She crossed the finish line, despite being accosted a few miles in by a race official who tried to tear off her bib number. Five years later, women were officially allowed to enter.

'Big Lil' – In 1968, three trawlers from Hull's fishing fleet sank in rapid succession in stormy conditions. Fishwife Lillian Bilocca from Hessle Road put down her filleting knife and embarked upon a campaign for better safety, marshalling support from the docks of Hull to Downing Street. She succeeded in changing the legislation, but along the way she was sacked from work, blacklisted by the fishing industry, mocked for her accent and sent death threats. Lil's story is documented in *The Headscarf Revolutionaries* (2015) by Brian W. Lavery, and I am indebted to Brian for his meticulous research. His book inspired this sequence.

'Tom Hulatt's Mile' – Tom Hulatt was an athlete from Tibshelf, Derbyshire who finished third behind Sir Christopher Chataway in the historic race of May 1954 that saw Roger Bannister run the first sub-four-minute mile. A miner at Williamthorpe colliery, he was the only runner in the race who was not a University student.

'Heinrich Harrer's Motorbike' – Harrer was an Austrian mountaineer best known for being part of the four-man team that made the first ascent of the North Face of the Eiger in 1938. He was a member of the Nazi party, though later disowned his involvement.

'Everest' – This poem touches upon the lives of several significant figures in the history of Himalayan mountaineering, including Beck Weathers and Lene Gammelgaard, both involved in the 1996 Everest disaster. Weathers spent a night in an open bivouac in a blizzard and miraculously survived. Gammelgaard was the first Scandinavian woman to summit Everest and has written about the fateful expedition in her book, *Climbing High*.

Acknowledgements

Some of the poems about female climbers first appeared in *Alpinist* magazine and in The Banff Centre's anthology *Rock, Paper, Fire*. The sequence about Alison Hargreaves started life during a residency in Banff and I am indebted to everyone at the Banff Centre for their support, particularly Marni Jackson and Tony Whittome. I am also particularly grateful to Katie Ives for her farsighted and keen eye, and for Ed Douglas for his advice.

Thanks are also due to the editors of *Poetry Review, Poetry London, Times Literary Supplement, The North, The Dark Horse, Route 57, Stand* and *Now Then,* where some of these poems first appeared.

'Murmuration' was a commissioned film-poem for Alistair Cook.

Thank you to The Society of Authors for a Roger Deakin Award which assisted with the research for this collection, and to the judges and trustees of the Fenton Aldeburgh Prize – some of these poems began on my writing week in Suffolk in 2015. Thank you to the University of Leeds and to Douglas Caster for granting me a two-year Cultural Fellowship which enabled the completion of this book as well as many other projects.

I am also grateful to Inntravel and Swiss Tourism for introducing me to the indomitable *Miss Jemima's Swiss Journal*, and for giving me the opportunity to spend a week in crinoline, following her footsteps in the Alps.

Some of this collection was also written during a two-year stint as Derbyshire Poet Laureate – thank you to Alison Betteridge and everyone at Derbyshire County Council for their support.

Personal thanks go to Alan Buckley, Ben Wilkinson, Andrew McMillan, Niall Fink, Parisa Ebrahimi, Ian Cartland, Hannah Copley, Jonathan Winter, Katie Ives, Kathy Towers, Ion Corcos, Miranda Pearson, A.B. Jackson, Les Robinson and Joe Hakim for advice and editing or for inspiring some of these pieces. Thanks also to the Thursday night poetry group at Leeds University School of English and to John Whale, and to Andrew Forster and everyone in our online workshop group.

Finally, thank you to everyone in Derbyshire Irregulars Climbing Society for all the routes, pints and limericks.